THE 90 DAY
BOOK BLUEPRINT

Unleash the
Best Seller
in You

The 90 Day Book Blueprint

By Derek DaVinci Chatman

THE 90-DAY

BOOK PROJECT

DEDICATION

This book is dedicated to all of the aspiring writers following their dream and pursuing their passion. I tip my hat to you and welcome you to this beautiful journey.

CHAPTERS

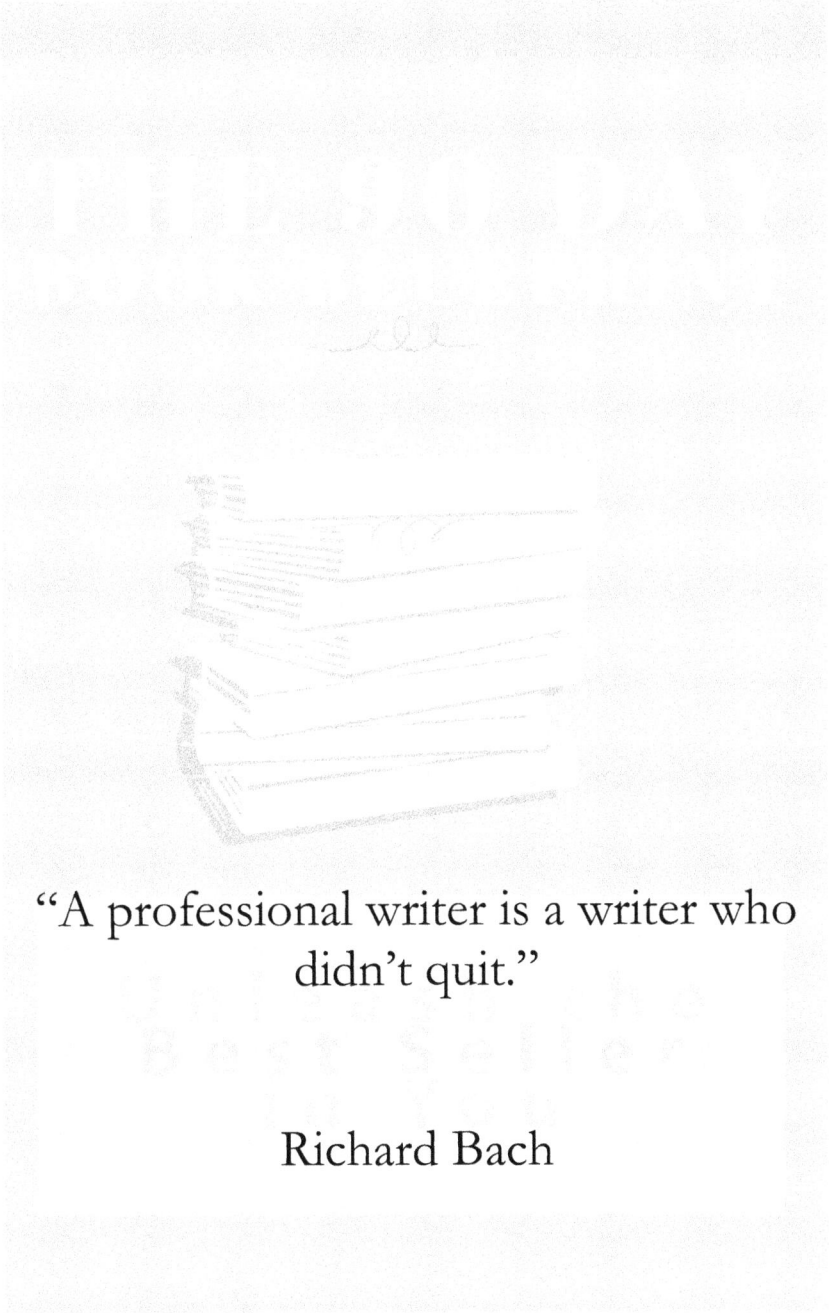

"A professional writer is a writer who didn't quit."

Richard Bach

Lesson 1: Getting Started

CONGRATS!!!

I want to say congratulations for taking this first step. For many, this will be the first stage in following your lifelong dream of becoming a professional writer! How awesome is that?! For others, this may be a one and done type deal. Your goal may be to write only one book. You may have a story to share and don't necessarily have interest in becoming a professional writer. This is equally awesome! I love both mindsets!

We will all have different goals and dreams, but in the end, we share one common ground. We all want to take the thoughts, stories and ideas in our head and transform them into a book.

Your wish is my command!

Consider me your personal genie in a bottle. I am here to help make your writing wishes come true. This book is designed to take the idea in your head and transform it into a book in your hand. I'm not going to lie, this book writing process will be a journey, but in the end you will be glad to have taken this trip with me. It will not be difficult. It will involve some discipline, focus, fun and imagination. In the end it will pay off. You will have written a book.

I was at this first stage exactly eight years ago. I had been dying to write a book for as long as I can remember. My biggest obstacles? I really didn't know how to get started and I was afraid I would fail. Despite my reservations and after years of failed attempts, one day I decided to take the plunge. I sucked it up, sat down in front of my laptop and began writing. I have to be honest. I made plenty of mistakes, but I also had plenty of victories and tons of growth. In the end, I accomplished my dream. I wrote a book. The feeling was absolutely awesome!

Since then, my books have taken me to places I could have never imagined. I've done speaking engagements, book signings and many book fairs. With that, I have gained fans all around the world. I swear I have to pinch myself sometimes to make sure I'm not dreaming. I would have never imagined that the pursuit of my dreams would inspire others to want to do the same. This brings me to today and to one of the most asked questions I receive when I attend events. Without fail, there is one reoccurring question that everyone asks.

"I've always wanted to write a book. How do I do it?"
This question pops up all of the time. I love to give advice and motivate and inspire budding writers to pursue their passion. I found myself mentoring other writers and spending hours answering questions about how I did it.

This sparked an idea. What if I took all that I've learned about book writing and put it into one central location where budding writers can have access to it at their fingertips? This is my motivation for creating this book and course. I want to help those who are interested in the "how to's'" of writing a book.

In my journey, I've studied the styles of some of the world's bestselling writers, from Stephen King, J.K Rowling, Donald Goines, Delia Owens, Mario Puzo, Paulo Coelho, Tolkien, Dan Brown, …. My list could go on for days. I took all of their great writing styles and habits and formulated them into this program. The goal? To help aspiring writers learn from the best of the best.

My ultimate goal is to lead you down the right path, to motivate you, inspire and steer you in the right direction, so you too can have your finished book in your hands.

With this guide, I want you to go and find a nice quiet place to sit back relax and chill. Get yourself a nice warm beverage and go on this journey with me. I promise to make this a no fluff, detailed yet simple, guide. When this is all done, the feeling is going to be unbelievable, euphoric! Wait until you see your name on the cover of your very own book!

WHO AM I ? WHY DID I CREATE THIS COURSE?

My name is Derek DaVinci Chatman and I like many of you, have always wanted to write a book. I don't have a fancy degree in English literature nor do I walk around with an ascot tucked in my collar and a tobacco pipe poking out of my mouth, while I spew lines from To Kill a Mockingbird. I'm just your average guy who had a big book idea floating around in my little head for as long as I can remember. I fumbled around with the idea of writing a book and made several half-hearted attempts before I eventually put the idea on the back burner.

Flash forward eight years, now I am the author of two book series and a self-improvement book. My first novel is a middle grade fantasy series called *The Legend of Virginia Smalls*. Concepts of this series had been bubbling in my head ever since the age of ten. I have to admit, it felt good to bring this story and its characters to life. There are currently three books in this series, with the fourth book coming soon.

My second novel is a Romantic suspense series called, *Dangerously in Love*. It's about a young bourgeois lady named Nia Wright, who falls in love with a dead man. I have two books in this series and I am currently putting the finishing touches on the third book.

My final book, which is actually my first book I have ever written and published, is called *Don't Be A Fool Go To School. Why College Is For You.* The entire plot of this book is in the books title. It's about going to college and pursuing your dreams. This is a passion project for me, because I returned to college later in life when I thought getting a degree was not possible. It's funny how things play out in life. This journey to pursue a college degree actually help re-ignite my interests in writing and finishing my book idea.

I started my book journey with zero book writing knowledge or skill. I was just the average guy living a middle class life with a wife and two young daughters. I grew up poor financially but not mentally. I had great parents and awesome brothers and sisters. We came up in what many would classify as the "hood" or the "projects" in a small yet colorful city called Springfield Massachusetts. I love every ounce of my upbringing because it made me who I am today. And boy did it enrich me with TONS of great stories and an abundance of characters.

The reason why I share this is because I want to let you know that it doesn't matter where you come from. If you set your mind to this book writing thing, you will get it done. Great stories and great books have no prejudice or any special qualifications, just your willingness to share it with the rest of the world. If I can do it, so can you.

Beaming with a little confidence, One day I grabbed my laptop and just started writing. I had no idea if I could do it. I just knew like most of you here know, I had a book in me and I wanted to express myself. In the beginning I put zero pressure on myself. This book writing thing would be my writing therapy. To heal and express that writer that lay dormant in me. This was my chance to transform myself from a caterpillar into a butterfly. Cheesy? Yeah, I know. But it's the truth. So what did I do? I kept it a secret. This was for me and for me only. If I never published it, that was fine with me. If the book sucked, then the world would never know. I just knew I had to get this done, no matter the odds.

I must admit, In the beginning I did have two things working in my favor. The first advantage, prior to writing my first book I had just finished an accelerated MBA program. The program was fast paced and I had to write school papers fast and against a timeline. This helped me with my focus because I was so used to doing a lot of writing based on a short deadline. My second advantage is the fact that I love, love, love good stories and I had a ton of them floating around in my head and I had the confidence enough to believe I could write. I think confidence is the biggest factor in any and everything. We all will have our advantages some different than others. Use them in your favor to write your book.

Now that you know a little bit about me, let's have some fun and delve deeper into this. It's going to be a great ride!

Lesson 2: How To Begin

"What are the two hardest steps in writing a book? Starting and finishing."

In the literary world, this quote captures the dilemma most budding writers face when first starting out. I've met hundreds of people who've told me they have an idea for a great book but they don't know where and how to start. Beneath the surface there is an underlying fear of the entire book writing process. I totally get it. Sharing the thoughts in your mind with others can be an intimidating thing. We can't discount it. It's real. We have to accept it for what it is and then learn how to get past it.

I have met quite a few people who've started writing a book and were several chapters deep into the process. I congratulate them and then as the conversation continues, I learn that they've been working on the book for several years and have no clear intention of ever finishing it.

Starting your book and finishing your book is what separates the novice writer from the professional. We all get busy in our hectic lives, however if we want a finished book, we have to make writing a priority. I can tell you first hand that you don't have to sacrifice the world to get your book written and finished. It takes some discipline and the right mindset. In this course I will provide some tip's that I believe will lead you to success.

So let's lay it all on the table, right now. If you are on the fence about writing your book, then you are probably thinking:

"Derek doesn't have a clue about my life and what I have going on right now." Your wrong. I know exactly what you are going through, because I've been there. I'm here to tell you, you can do it. I want to put these myths to rest so we can start writing. I've come up with a list of the top excuses we use that hold us back from writing our book. Are you using any of them?

The top excuses that hold us back from writing our book:
1. I don't have the time to write.
2. I'm not a good writer. No one will take me serious.
3. What if my book sucks?

We have all been here. We have all had our doubts, but you can't let that stop you. They are all untrue. You are here because you have a story to share and you have a passion for writing. Let that be your guide. Let that be your shining light.

Excuse# 1: I don't have time to write.
This is probably the biggest excuse. We all have busy lives. We may work a full time job, have a family, work crazy shifts and don't have time in our busy day to sit down and write for several hours. Even if we do find a moment of freedom, we are exhausted from all of our daily activities. I was so in this boat when I started writing my first book. At one point I was working third shift in a factory for twelve hours a day. I have a wife

and young children and I didn't want to take away quality time with them. So how did I do it? I made the time. I had to carve out personal writing time for myself. You have to do it. You deserve it.

I would take my laptop to work with me and work during my lunch breaks. I would take an hour or two at home before the family woke up for the day. (Early mornings ensured some quietness). I've written chapters while on vacation in Florida with the family. We always rent a house near Disney World. While my family swam in the pool, I spent an hour or so typing away before I put my laptop down and joined them in the water. If you have a free hour or two great, if not steal some time to get your writing done. You have to be creative. You can write in the car while waiting in the parking lot while your children are at Soccer practice. You can type away while waiting for your hair appointment at your hairdressers salon. You can type away while sitting on the toilet. How you do it is totally up to you, Be creative. Find your time.

It's important to remember, not all days are going to be awesome productive days and that's ok. To be honest, there are days where I only write a paragraph. That's absolutely fine, because if I stay consistent, after a while one paragraph turns into two and two paragraphs turn into three and three paragraphs turn into a page and before you know it, I've written an entire chapter.

Even today, I will grab my laptop, crawl into bed and write a paragraph and then close the laptop before calling it a night. This keeps the momentum going and before you know it, in a week you almost finished a chapter.

In the best case scenario, If you have the time to write. Find a quiet place to sit down, preferably a place with a window that you can gaze out of when you need to gather your thoughts. This can be a spare bedroom or an office in your home, dedicated to writing. When I first started writing, I was at the kitchen table right next to the window that looked out into our wooded backyard. I wrote early in the morning before anyone in my house had a chance to wake up. If you can't get a totally quiet room, try wearing headphones. Play something that relates or sets the mood to your story. Try to play something without words or on low, so it plays as the backdrop or soundtrack to your book. You would be absolutely amazed how well this works. Boy, does music help set a mood for a story!

EXCUSE# 2: I'm not a good writer. No one will take me serious.

Don't get me wrong, writing takes skill. But you don't have to be an English major or someone who is a walking dictionary to write a book. When I think professional writer, I used to think of the stereotypical smug characters we see in movies. You know, the guy in the cardigan sweater, smoking pipe, typewriter and perfectly trimmed beard. Of course writers come in every shape, color, size, gender, sexual orientation and religious belief.

It's not our task to be perfect little walking dictionaries or follow silly stereotypes. This is what a good editor is for. They can come in and clean up mistakes and typo's. I don't care who you are, when you write you are going to have errors. We are all human, so don't let that slow you down.

Even great writers like, J.K Rowling and Stephen King have editors. All of the professionals do. It's part of the process.

For me, I often leave out words when I write. It's like my mind glosses over and fills in the blanks. An editor will catch simple errors like this and fix them for you. I will cover editors later on in this course. And please don't be frightened, in today's technological world, an editor can be found easily and very affordable.

I believe the biggest element in writing is your ability to tell a good compelling story. If you can do this, your readers will love you. Readers love well written, memorable characters and stories. They want to be swept up and taken into your universe. You have a unique voice and unique story, so tell it.

While you are writing, I would recommend you keep what you are doing to yourself. Don't share it with your friends, mom, dad, children, neighbors or co-workers. This is about you and for you only. At this point. You are writing for yourself. If you view it this way. It will make the process easier.

Now, if you are married, you may have to share it with your spouse because you live together but if you can keep it on the hush until you are finished, that would be great. I am an energy person. I love to keep the energy in my life positive. Sometimes our loved ones try to protect us and they will put their fears and energy on us. We don't need any of that. So if you can, keep the book on the hush.

Now, my wife is one of the most supportive people I know, but I didn't tell her I was writing a book until I had the completed book in my hand. This was not about her, it was about me. Of course I love her but I needed to prove it to myself, first. I wanted the proof to be in the pudding and it was. I remember walking up to her with my completed, self-published book in my hand. I handed it to her and said "Hey, I wrote a book." She looked absolutely shocked. Till this day, she wonders how and when I did it. Of course I had just finished my Master's Degree, so my wife assumed I was still writing for school so she never questioned why I was at my laptop typing away.

Excuse# 3: What If My Book Sucks?

I love this excuse, because it's the most honest of them all. Let's say, you have all your ducks in a row and you've written your book. You are going to have people who read it and absolutely love it and you will have people who absolutely hate it. But it will not suck. I promise. If you write a compelling story the readers will come.

Good and bad reviews are part of the game. Remember, you are one of a kind and very unique. This means you will have a unique voice and writing style that will attract readers. You have a story to tell. Trust me, you have no clue how your writing will touch someone's life, so don't worry about not being taken seriously or sucking. Some people love pizza, some people hate it. Some people love broccoli. I personally can't stand it. To each their own. Our job is to write and attract those who love our style. They are out their waiting for your book. Go get them!

Let me tell you, a finished book automatically sparks credibility and respect. It's like telling someone you climbed Mount Everest. When in actuality, all you did was take one step at a time and before you knew it, you were standing at the mountain top.

I found some motivation to write my first book after I found out a family member had published a book. It inspired me to do the same and in turn, my books have motivated many people to follow their dreams. The best feeling in the world is when someone tells me they love my book and they can't wait for the next one. Or even better when they tell me my book has motivated them to write their own book. Don't be afraid. It's time to share your book with the world.

Lesson 3: Creating Your Outline

We have all the excuses out in the open and out of our way. Now, let's get down to the nitty gritty. I'm sure if you're taking this course, you are here because you already have a general idea of what you want to write. If not, this would be the perfect time to brainstorm.

There are some key things to focus on. What is the main plot of the book? Who are your characters? Who is the protagonist? Who or what is the antagonist? Is there a conflict in the story? What will our characters go or grow through? These are the basics, however it is very important to take time to think this out. It is also important to write them down. I have set aside space in this book to record your ideas. However, feel free to write on another file in your computer or you can write them down on a separate sheet of paper. It is important to go through this exercise before you start because it will give you a great place to reference back to when you write. You will be surprised how easy it is to forget character names and personalities and how easy it is to venture off of the main theme. Your outline is your bible. It will keep you on task. Now please understand, book writing is fluid. What we start in an outline can change in the course of the book.

When you list your characters, feel free to add details like, name, age, gender, race, personality, etc… all the little things that define who they are. Plot out your book below.

BOOK OUTLINE

Main character (s)

Protagonist

Antagonist

Main Plot of the book

What will the characters go or grow through?

Setting

This outline is a simple format I use for all of my books. There are no rules in outlining. It is for your use only. So feel free to add as much detail to this outline as you need to help guide you. Also when you are not writing is usually the time when good ideas about your story will come to you. RECORD THEM! This is very important. Jot them down on a scrap piece of paper or record them on your phone. Do whatever it takes to save and capture them. Then when you have a chance, add them to your outline. This is key. Many great ideas go forgotten once time has passed. Of course, my ideas usually come to me in the shower. So after cleaning up, I immediately add them to the notes section on my phone. Then I transfer them to my outline when I get back to my computer.

PLOTTERS VS SEAT OF THE PANTSERS

When creating your outline, in the writing world, there are generally two types of writers. There are the "Plotters" and the "Seat of the Pants" style of writers. Plotters LOVE detail and love to plot out the entire story from beginning to end. This is done before they even begin to write. They will outline a list of all character names, ways of dress, personalities, family tree, book locations, dates, what will happen in each individual chapter. The ending, background story, etc… A plotter could have pages and pages of detailed notes before they even start to write. This level of detail can make the writing process easy and focused.

JK Rowling, the writer of the Harry Potter book series, is an infamous outline plotter. Before writing, she will have detailed sketching's of characters, names and locations, plot points along with the beginning and ending of the story. Her level of detail is remarkable. She pretty much has a great chunk of the story all ready to go. Now all she has to do is formulate it into the story. The only caution I offer to the Plotter, is to make sure you don't spend all of your time plotting and never begin to write because you don't have the entire story written out in your outline.

Now for the "Seat of the Pants" style of writer, the name says it all. They love to fly by the seat of their pants. They will have a small detailed outline and they let the story come to them and through them. They have a general idea of how the story is going to flow, but they do not go into much detail when they write the outline. Stephen King, the author of Carrie and The Green Mile is a "Seat of the Pants" style of writer. He likes to let the story come to him. He is more interested in character and situation and following them where they take him. Often times, he has no idea what will happen to the characters in the end. They could live or they could die. It's like unfolding a mystery in your head.

I personally, am a "Seat of the Pants" style of writer. I will have a general idea of the plot as well as characters names and the journey the will go through but I LOVE to let the characters personalities and story come to me as I write. The only caution I offer to the "Seat of the Pants" outliner, is to make sure you stay focused and on task. Without much structure, it is easy to take your story on a tangent away from the main theme.

There is value in both styles of writers. Take time to discover your writing and outlining style. You have lived with yourself your entire life, so I am sure you have a pretty good idea what style works best for you. Don't force yourself into being something you are not. This can lead to frustration and stall you from writing your story.

You may discover that you are actually a combination of both styles. That's absolutely fine. Remember the outline is a tool to help you write your story, nothing more, nothing less.

Once completed, make sure you keep this outline with you whenever you write. It should be easily assessable and right at your fingertips.

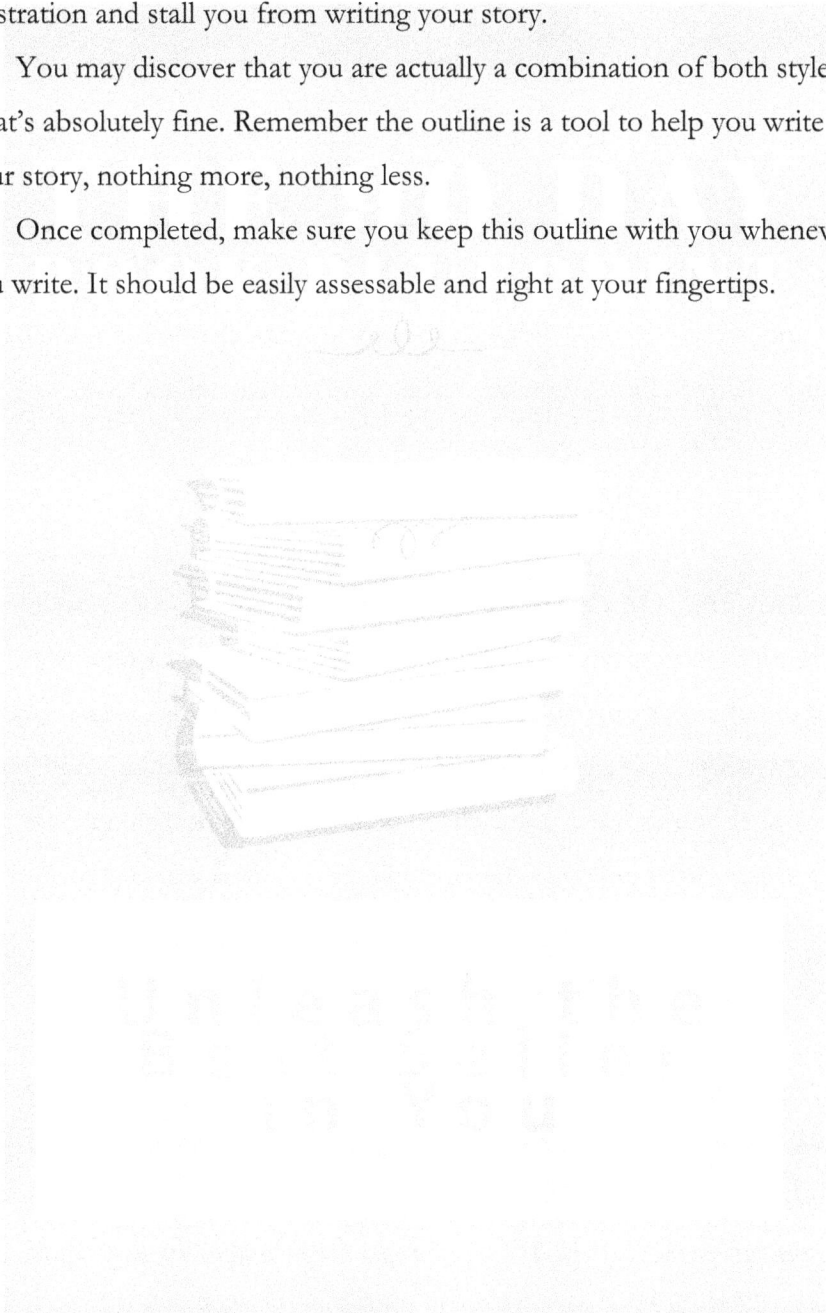

Lesson 4: Finding Your Writing Style

Now that you have your outline, let's go into more detail about your writing style. When you're first starting out, I would recommend modeling after one of your favorite writers. Let me add some clarity. I'm not talking about plagiarism. Don't write what they have written and call it your own. Read several pages of their book or close your eyes and listen to their words in an audiobook. Do they write in first person? Is everything coming from the mind of the character? Do they write in third person, more like a birds eye view or a God mode where you know the thoughts and actions of every character? Does your favorite writer or writers use a lot of descriptive words? How do they present their words? Understanding writing styles is both and art and a science. Do this a few minutes before you write or you can read a few chapters or the entire book(s) in your spare time. It will put you in the right mindset. Here is a paragraph from Mario Puzo's the Godfather. I absolutely love the way he describes one of the main characters, Michael Corleone, in the early pages of the book.

"Michael Corleone was the youngest son of the Don and the only child who refused the great man's direction. He did not have the heavy, Cupid-shaped face of the other children, and his jet black hair was straight rather than curly. He was handsome in a delicate way. Indeed there had been a time when the Don had worried about his youngest

son's masculinity. A worry put to rest when Michael Corleone became
seventeen years old."

In this one paragraph, Mario Puzo does an awesome job of giving not just a physical description of Michael, but his choice of words give you some background and history of the main character and his relation to his siblings and his father Don Corleone. At the end it leaves you with a little bit of mystery about the main character. What happened to Michael when he was seventeen? Mario Puzo leaves the reader wanting more.

Now let's take a look at "Harry Potter and the Philosopher's Stone" written by JK Rowling. Look at how JK Rowling introduces the readers to Harry Potter for the first time. I love this introduction.

"Dudley's favourite punch-bag was Harry, but he couldn't often catch
him. Harry didn't look it, but he was very fast. Perhaps it had something
to do with living in a dark cupboard, but Harry had always been small
and skinny for his age. He looked even smaller and skinnier than he
really was because all he had to wear were old clothes of Dudley's and
Dudley was about four times bigger than he was. Harry had a thin face,
knobby knees, black hair and bright green eyes. He wore round glasses
held together with a lot of Sellotape because of all the times Dudley had
punched him on the nose. The only thing Harry liked about his own
appearance was a very thin scar on his forehead which was shaped like a
bolt of lightning."

In this one paragraph, JK Rowling does an unbelievable job describing

Harry's iconic look, but at the same time, can you see the beauty in the way she interweaved Harry's relationship with Dudley? Not only was Harry bullied by Dudley, the description gives Harry's pecking order in the Dudley household. I love it!!

Mario Puzo and JK Rowling have different styles of writing but they both have a great way of painting a picture in their readers mind. In both reading examples, JK Rowling and Mario Puzo are both descriptive but they keep it beautiful yet simple.

Now please make sure you don't get caught up in trying to use words and descriptions to sound fancy for fancies sake. It can alienate and bore your reader. I love my thesaurus just like every other writer, but use words that you and your characters would use in their normal conversations.

This drives me absolutely insane. I get frustrated when I have to read a sentence over three or four times just to understand what the writer is trying to express. Keep the words beautiful yet simple. It will keep your readers engaged and wanting more. You will lose them if they don't understand what you're talking about. Despite what anyone may tell you, the reader is first. They are your audience. You almost want to make the reading so fluid that the reader forgets that they are even reading. You want them to get lost deep inside your story.

Once you've modeled for a while and you get deeper into your writing project, you will start to discover your own personal style. You will find your own voice in the way you engage and entertain your readers.

Lesson 5: **Writing Your First Chapter**

Now we have our outline and understanding of our writing style, lets write our first chapter. The first paragraph and chapter can be deemed by many as the most important part of your book. Why? Because this is where you want to grab and captivate your reader and never let them go. If your first chapter is terrible, you could lose your readers. Make sure this chapter begins with a bang that keeps your readers wanting to read more.

Let's take a look at Gillian Flynn's novel "Gone Girl". Her introduction is beautiful. It's odd, yet interesting and it leaves the reader wanting to read more.

"When I think of my wife, I always think of her head. The shape of it to begin with. The very first time I saw her, it was the back of the head I saw and there was something lovely about it. The angles of it. Like a shiny hard corn cornel or a riverbed fossil. She had what the Victorians would call a finely shaped head. You can imagine the skull quite easily. I'd know her head anywhere and what's inside it. I think of that too. Her mind, her brain, all those coils and her thoughts shuttling through those coils like fast frantic centipedes. Like a child, I picture opening her skull, unspooling her brain and sifting through it, trying to catch and pin down her thoughts."

This intro grabs the reader and sets sort of a dark tone of the main character, Nick Dunne, who is accused of murdering his wife. Gillian Flynn wastes no time getting right to the point and getting into the dark yet precocious mind of her main character. It pulls you right in to the story.

Think about the genre you are writing for. Think about your readers and what they like and what would interest them. At the same time, deliver your unique story, regardless of what the reader thinks. Does this sound like a contradiction? Well, it truly is. That's the delicate balance of writing. It's like know all the rules of your genre but at the same time be willing to break every single one of them while trying to maintain the sanctity of your genre. There is no penalty for writing a romance novel and the main character turns into a zombie. Ok, I'm being a little extreme here because I am trying to make a point. These are books and you have unlimited resources. There are no boundaries. Let your mind be free.

We Captivated our Reader, Now What's Next?

OK now our first chapter is done and we have captivated our reader and they want to read more. Please, please, continue to build that momentum of excitement and intrigue. Keep your story interesting. Leave EVERY chapter with the reader wanting more. Leave them with some little mini cliff hangers, something to make them say "What?" I need to read more to find out what's going to happen next.

Consistency is key when you're writing. Like I mentioned earlier, make the time to write. Go to your designated writing space, grab your warm beverage and start your first chapters. Like everything, you have to build momentum. You are not going to have a complete book in a day. You have to start with the first step. Like building a house, you have to start with the first brick. If you stay consistent then before you know it, you will have a finished book. An ideal day of writing should be about two hours. This is a good amount of time before you go batty. If you can't do two hours at once then make sure you steal a little time during the day. You could wake up an hour before the family and spend forty five minutes to an hour writing. Steal some time, say writing thirty minutes after dinner or you could spend thirty minutes to an hour writing before bedtime. These are all simple examples. Be creative, find your writing space and time. Make it happen.

Make sure you are passionate about what you do. Have fun with this. Don't make it a chore. When it's a chore, there is no fun in it and you will try to avoid writing. With that being said, you will indeed have days where it will indeed feel like a task instead of writing. In this case, take a small break and come back to it. When you write, the best material comes from you when you are focused and open. With that being said, this is just the first draft of your book. Don't be afraid to write crap this first go around. As you write more and gain experience, even your crap will be pretty decent writing. Write the thoughts that come to you. Don't be afraid. This does not have to be perfect. We will come back around and clean things up. You will thank me in the end.

OK, let's flow. Let's get those first chapters on the page! In order to keep a deadline, I challenge myself with small goals. Let's say we are going to write a 200 page novel. For a 6 x 9 inch book, that would equal about

55,000 words. If you are typing in a word document then it will count your words and pages for you. I don't want you to obsess on the numbers. We are going to use them as a guide to help us achieve our goals, nothing more, nothing less. There are many software templates you can use for writing. You can use a traditional Word document from Microsoft. If you go to KDP.amazon.com, (which is Kindle Direct Publishing's website and the self-publishing platform used by Amazon). On there you can download a free Word writing template you can use to write your book. It's free and It comes in a variety of book sizes. Take a moment and look at your favorite books and determine what book size works for you.

There are also excellent writing programs like Scrivener, Evernote, Ywriter that give you much more writing options. Take some time and research what options work best for you. Make sure whatever you choose, it is not too complicated for you. We don't want to spend too much time dallying with a writing program. Me personally I use Word and Scrivener.

WEEK # 1

Day 1-2: Write your opening paragraph.

Day 3-4: Write your first page.

Day 5-7: Finish your first five pages.

Follow this guide and stay disciplined. If you find yourself in a flow and are super motivated, please continue to write past your daily goals. Don't stop if you are motivated.

I am starting with a slow build. In two days, you will have plenty of time to write a paragraph. Then after that you have two days to write your first page. The momentum builds a bit but by the end of the week you will have five pages. That would average to about three quarters of a page a day. Not too bad at all! On your goal sheet, I want you to cross off each milestone you reach. Now let's move on to week #2.

WEEK # 2

Day 1-2: Let's write four pages.

Day 3-4: Let's write another four pages.

Day 5-7: Lets ramp up the momentum. Write five pages.
             For a total page count of 18 pages in two weeks.

In between your writing, make sure you take time to think about your story. This is key. Do this every day before you sit down to write. If you are a "Seat of the Pantser" let the story come to you. If you are "Plotter", you've probably already written down where you want to go with the story. Even as a Plotter, you can still think about the story, how it will develop and how you will deliver it to your readers. You want to have a plan of where you want to go with the story before you write each day. This doesn't have to be formal. I do my thinking in the shower or I will take a walk and run ideas through my head. You can do this in the car or on the train on your commute to work. All you need is about five to ten free minutes to think and plot your story. Also before you write, go back and reread what you wrote yesterday. Don't obsess and try to fix everything. Feel free to let typo's go for now. We are rereading what we wrote yesterday to keep us in the same flow of writing. Do this every day before you write.

WEEK # 3

We are going to increase the momentum a bit. We are now three weeks into this. You should be getting used to writing about 2 pages in a day. Please remember to take time to think of the next phases of your story, before your write.

Day 1-2: Let's write four pages.

Day 3-4: Let's write another five pages.

Day 5-7: Lets ramp up the momentum. Write six pages.
For a total page count of 33 pages in three weeks.

This pace may feel a little crazy with writing a page or two a day. You are a writer now, so you have to stay committed. Just think, the best-selling authors are writing eight hours a day. We are doing this in 1-3 hours per day. Not bad. Find your focus and continue writing. How does it feel? How do you feel about your story so far? If you feel something is missing or don't like how things are unfolding, if you have time, go back and make a few tweaks. This is absolutely ok. Like I said earlier, this writing process is fluid. The story can change as you write. That is the beauty in this process.

WEEK # 4

We are reaching the home stretch and finishing our first full month of writing. Congrats! This is awesome! I want you to celebrate this victory. Treat yourself to something nice. A nice glass of wine (if you're of legal age) or a nice dinner out on the town. Do whatever makes you smile. You've earned it. The final week of this month is going to be similar to Week # 3.

Day 1-2: Let's write five pages.

Day 3-4: Let's write another six pages.

Day 5-7: Lets ramp up the momentum. Write eight pages. For a total page count of 52 pages in four weeks.

After your first full month as a writer, you have 52 pages completed. Books sizes can vary, but you could be about 3-6 chapters into your book. Make sure your chapter titles relate to the subject in the chapter. If you have a reveal or plot twist in the chapter make sure you don't reveal it with the chapters heading. We want to surprise our readers. Sounds silly but this is an easy rookie mistake to make.

WEEK # 5

Remember to stay consistent. Find the time to write and plot your next pages in your book. You will have distractions and things that come up that alter your writing schedule. Stay diligent. Find the time and make it happen. Make sure you are referencing your outline to see if you are staying on pace. Give your readers a good amount of information to keep the story compelling. However, don't overdue and bore the reader with unnecessary excessive information.

Day 1-2: Let's write five pages.

Day 3-4: Let's write another six pages.

Day 5-7: Write eight pages. For a total page count of 71 pages in five weeks.

WEEK # 6

We have reached our sixth week. If you find yourself ahead in page count, congrats! If a little bit of life got in the way and you are behind, it's ok. The page count is only a guideline. You will have time to catch up before our ninety days arrives. Maybe sneak in an extra paragraph or two a day to catch up.

Day 1-2: Let's write five pages.

Day 3-4: Let's write another six pages.

Day 5-7: Write eight pages. For a total page count of 90 freaking pages in week six!!

Lesson 6: Developing The Middle of Your Story

Congratulations you've made it to another milestone. We've made it to the middle of our book! I don't want to jinx things, especially since we have built so much momentum these past few weeks. In the middle is where we have to maintain the most focus. We have to stay consistent with our writing because the middle of a book is where most writers quit.

There is a valid reason why we stall at the midpoint of our writing journey. It has nothing to do with a lack of dedication or writers block. It has everything to do with the natural art of story-telling.

When we have a great book idea, we generally have the subject and how we want our book to begin. We may have an ending in mind as well. This is both a gift and a curse. A gift that we know how to begin and end our book. The curse is, filling the middle of our book with a compelling story. For most of us, we have no clue of where to go with the middle. This is the substance of our book, the meat and potatoes. This is where the fun begins. We have to figure a way to tie the beginning of our story to our end.

Take some time and think about your characters. Where do you want them to go? What challenges will they face? Will they have to sacrifice something to reach our great ending? Remember you have unlimited resources when writing a book. Think out of the box, be creative, be bold, be different, be exciting.

Let's ramp things up and build on the excitement. We started our book with a bang and we will end it with a bang. So naturally, we must have a bang in the middle of our book, as well. In the novel, The Godfather by Mario Puzo, the book is a great example of having a compelling beginning, middle and ending. (Let me warn you there are Godfather spoilers ahead. Yes, I know the Godfather is over fifty years old and the story has been made into a movie and is part of pop culture. I hate when a great story is spoiled.)

The book starts with a nice bang. We get to experience all of Don Corleone's power and influence in the underground world of the mafia. The wedding of the Don's daughter Connie, is the most poignant part of the beginning of the book. Why? Because we get to see many people come to the Don for his help. It gives a barometer of his power and influence.

Now the ending ends with a bang when Michael Corleone assumes the throne of his father's empire by getting vengeance on all of his father's enemies. This sounds like an awesome beginning and ending to me. I'm sure Mario Puzo had these two concepts in his mind before he began writing the book. So how did he get from a great beginning to a great ending? How did he build on the momentum?

It was the middle of his book. The middle follows quiet, unassuming Michael Corleone into his rise to power. We get to see his character shift from a modest, even tempered baby brother to a ruthless Don. We soon discover out of all of the siblings, Michael is the most similar to his father. It is the development of Michael's character in the middle of the book that makes the story compelling.

So with this in mind. Let's get to the middle of our book.

WEEK # 7

Remember consistency is the key. Let's get really creative in these middle chapters. The pages per day are a guideline. If on day one our two you feel like writing more than five pages, go for it. Or let's say day 3-4, you were busy and had no time to write. You can make it up later in the week. You may even write most of your pages on the weekend and do no writing during the week. That is fine too. You have to find what works best for you and your situation. In the end though, we want to reach our writing goal.

Day 1-2: Let's write five pages.

Day 3-4: Let's write another six pages.

Day 5-7: Write eight pages. For a total page count of 109 pages in seven weeks.

Now let's proceed to week 8.

We are in the heat of battle. We are at the center of our story. It is important to be passionate about this project. Let's focus on our characters. Characters are VERY important when writing your book. It's easy to fall into the trap of making them stereotypical or one dimensional. Make sure you give your characters distinct personalities. After all, we are all very distinct in real life. Also remember, your villain is just as, if not more important to your story than your hero. Readers love to hate the villain. Luke Skywalker was awesome in Star Wars but the real intrigue and magic came from Darth Vader. We love a brave hero like Frodo in the Lord Of The Rings, but the challenge to keep the ring out of the hands of Gollum makes the story and the journey worth our while.

We can even mix it up and have heroes and villains we love and hate all at the same time. The Game of Thrones series does an excellent job at playing with our emotions. At times I am in love with Daenerys Targaryen and then there are moments where I think she's absolutely awful. The same can be said for Jaime and Cersei Lannister. They made my skin crawl but at the same time, I found moments where I empathized with them. Now John Snow and Arya Stark can do no wrong in my mind, but that is a whole other story within itself.

My final remarks on characters would be, pour your emotions into them as much as you can, use the personalities and attributes of the people you've encountered in life into these characters. The reason why this is critical? Because of the emotional connection you have with others. Describe how they make you feel within your character interactions.

Readers love characters that draw an emotional reaction. It will add some realness and depth to your characters and your story. Ps. If you base a character on a person you know, make sure you change the name. This will make Thanksgiving dinner really awkward, if you don't.

I've used my personal experiences with many of my characters. Some of the best experiences and characterizations come from personal feelings and personal pain. I used to be a very anxious person, you better believe I have characters who go through it themselves. It's like I leave a little piece of me in every book.

To end this section on character, don't be afraid to kill off a character. I know we grow attached to them and they are a part of us, however if it is to build our story. We have to do it. I have to be honest, I have had serious dilemmas with killing off characters and it hurt, but boy the readers reactions were both heartfelt and amazing.

Here are our writing goals for week #8

Day 1-2: Let's write six pages.

Day 3-4: Let's write another eight pages.

Day 5-7: Write eight pages. For a total page count of 131 pages in eight weeks.

WEEK # 9

We are getting closer. We are now over two months into our writing process and close to three quarters of our book is completed. If you have come to the stumbling point many like to call "Writers Block" there are simple ways to get through it. For the record, I don't believe in writers block. It's just a little pause in creativity. Put your pen down and go for a walk. Think about the story and where you want it to go. Think, think think!! I recommend letting the story come to you. Don't force it and don't be afraid to venture down many avenues in your mind to enrich your story. Some of the best ideas come when we are not afraid to venture out of our comfort zones and fixed ways of thinking. Remember you are the story teller and the universe builder. So build an intriguing world that our readers would love to get caught up in. Listen to your inner voice and listen to your characters. If you listen without distractions, I swear they will speak to you and then through you.

Here are our writing goals for week# 9

Day 1-2: Let's write seven pages.

Day 3-4: Let's write another eight pages

Day 5-7: Write eight pages. For a total page count of 154 pages in nine weeks.

Lesson 7: Finishing Your Story

We are nearing the finish line. We've made it to over 150 pages and are fifty pages closer to our goal. Congratulations, you've made it further than most people who set their sights out in writing a book. I remember reading somewhere that 97% of people who begin writing a book, never finish. The morning before writing this section of this book, I read a post on social media about this young lady who said she started writing her book eight years ago and would love to finish. Boy could she use this program!

I know some of you taking this course are probably in this boat. You started, life got in the way and you've never finished. The characters in my head would drive me insane if I never gave them a conclusion.

This failure to finish can at times be attributed to our goal of trying to write the perfect book. We don't trust our talent and we doubt our writing instincts. This leads to an incomplete quest and an eternal dragging of our feet. This is our first run through. I promise it is not going to be perfect. Guess what? No one has read the book so far, except you. It's not a finished product. It's like taking the turkey out of the oven an hour before it's done and expecting it to taste good.

This is our little book universe. We can go back, change, add and remove all types of things to make our final story.

Prior to writing a book, I would have never thought I would say this next sentence. I love the rewriting and editing part of the process. The reason why? Because now I know the entire story. I can go back, change names, adjust personalities, add more pop to my story. We can do a multitude of things to make sure in the end we have a book that we love. Let's venture into week 10 of our book writing process.

WEEK # 10

Let's make sure our story comes full circle. Let's go out with a bang! This doesn't necessarily mean a dramatic ending (which I love, too), it can be an ending that brings our characters and our readers to a resolution. Be crafty about this. We don't want to fizzle at our end. Our reader should put the book down and feel a sense of completion. They should feel like the story has been completely told and they are fine with the final resolution.

Have we obtained the goal and theme of our book? Were we able to capture our vision? This is the time to start planning to land this plane. We have to begin to tie loose ends. It is important to have good pacing. Nothing drives a reader more crazy if our story telling is on level 100 and we abruptly end the story right at the peak, leaving our readers unsatisfied.

Like the end of the Harry Potter book series. Without trying to reveal any spoilers, Harry's story comes to a satisfying conclusion. He and the other characters in the book have grown, learned lessons and are better, more powerful people in the end. The journey that they set out in the beginning of the book has been accomplished. Not all the good guys win in the end. However if they lose, there is a reason being and it is our job as writers to make sure our readers understand this.

Ok, let's get to writing our week number 10.

WEEK# 10 Continued

Day 1-2: Let's write seven pages.

Day 3-4: Let's write another eight pages

Day 5-7: Write eight pages. For a total page count of 177 pages in ten weeks.

WEEK # 11

We are rounding the bases and ready to run into home plate and score. Let's stay focused with our goal in our mind. Stay diligent with all of the things we talked about in week ten. Let's give this book a great ending. Let's make sure all of our stories are complete and we have tied loose ends. Keep the momentum going. Keep following your writing schedule. We are mere pages from our end.

Ok, let's get to writing our week number 11.

Day 1-2: Let's write seven pages.

Day 3-4: Let's write another eight pages

Day 5-7: Write eight pages. For a total page count of 200 pages in eleven weeks.

Lesson 8: The Conclusion

We did it!! We finished our book!! I knew you had it in you! I knew you could do it! It took some discipline but you are now amongst the top three percent of people who started writing their book and finished it.

So now that we have spent weeks in a writing frenzy, what do we do next? We are going to take a dramatic turn. I want you to close your laptop, put down your pen and pad and forget about the book. Yes seriously. For the next two days, I don't want you to think about the book. Give your brain a break. Why? Because we are going to read the book over and I want your mind to be recalibrated. I want you to re-read your book under fresh new eyes. If you have the discipline and don't mind stretching the book writing process, then you can take an entire week off.

After our hiatus, we are going to come back to our book and put the finishing touches on it.

Let's edit our book. We are going to work on the final draft. Now if you followed my guidance, this process should be fun and not difficult or time consuming. We are going to run through, edit grammar issues or parts of the story that don't make sense.

After we make it through our final draft, how do you feel? Listen to your gut. Do you feel good about what you've written? If a part of the story doesn't feel right, then don't be afraid to change it. This is the time

Lesson 9: What Do I Do Next?

So, what do we do next? Your book is officially finished and we are ready to take it to the next level, the ultimate level. We want to put our book in the hands of our readers. This is an awesome situation to be in. Here is where we have to decide what route works best for us. As I mentioned earlier, there are typically two routes to take. Do we go Traditional publishing or do we go the Self-publishing route?

The first route is the traditional route, which consists of submitting your work to a Literary agent, who will in-turn represent you and submit your work to a publisher. In this case your completed book is now technically a manuscript that will be shopped to publishers.

The second route you can take with your finished book is the self-publishing route. This is a new route that was not available to writers some eight to ten years ago. With the birth of the digital age and platforms like Amazon Kindle, Apple iBook, Barnes & Noble Press and Kobo to name a few, writers are now taking creative control of their projects. With either option, there are pros and cons associated with both opportunities. Let's explore them.

With going with a traditional publisher, the first pro is the validation factor. You did it. A traditional publisher has officially put their stamp of approval on your work and you are officially a writer. With traditional publishers there are no upfront costs. They will do everything for you in regards to getting your book out to the public. All you have to do is write, submit and go on tour. Of course, it is a lot more complicated than that but you get the gist. The traditional publishers have been doing this book thing since forever, so they know how to market your book and reach your target audience. You let the professionals handle the work. In most publishing deals you will get paid an advance and a percentage of every book sold.

Of course this also comes with a negative side or a con. As a writer you may have to give up some of your creative control when you go the traditional route. The publisher can have creative rights over your book. They view your work as both an art and a business. On principle, there is nothing necessarily wrong with this, however you may have to compromise some of your personal style and opinion for their expert opinion. They know what sells and how to capture their audience. For example, you may have one idea for a book cover and your literary agent and publisher may have another idea that they feel better captures the audience and essence of the book. This is all part of their creative control once they agree to publish your book. This is not always the case, however you have to be willing to understand how the system works. Even the great Joanne Rowling was asked to use her initials, J.K Rowling on the book cover of her Harry Potter books because they felt boys wouldn't want to read the book if it was written by a woman. Were they correct? We will never know, however the series went on to sell millions of books.

You can also expect lower royalty fees going the traditional route. They can be in the range of 6-10% depending on your deal. It is a small cut over the overall books sales but this is understood in the industry because the publisher is fronting all of the costs and covering all of the expenses. You will also have to account for the percentage you will have to pay your literary agent. Your literary agent will get a certain percentage of your commissions, which is usually in the range of 15%. There are also royalties your publisher will pay you when your book sells. They own the rights to your book, so you may get paid an upfront fee called an advance and you will only make 6-10% percent off of each book sold. You can potentially leave a lot of money on the table if you go with a traditional publisher.

If traditional publishing doesn't work for you, the other option is self-publishing your book yourself. There a pros in this. For one, you will have total control of the entire process. All creative ideas will come from you. You will not have to worry about rejection letters from publishers and literary agents because there will be no gate keeper standing in between you and your readers. You publish when and how you want, no questions asked. Publishing yourself will also give you higher royalties. In some cases it can be between 50 and 90%, depending on the distribution channel you choose to go with to publish your book. You can use print on demand services like Amazon. This means you don't have to have a giant stock on hand when selling your books. Services like Amazon, will only print your book when a customer orders it on their website. This can save you tons of money. You will also have the option of selling your book as an e-book download.

Of course all of this sounds great, but there are cons to self-publishing. With the freedom of having total control of your project also means you will have to wear many hats and do a lot of things yourself beyond the writing. You will be in this alone so you have to get your own cover design, find the right distribution channel, market your book, find an editor. This will come at a cost to you. All out of your own pocket. Unlike traditional publishing, you will have to pay for all of these services upfront, yourself.

Now don't get nervous all of this can be done pretty cheap. Depending on your skill level a book can cost you between $200-$1,500 to make. There are tons of freelancers out there that can help you with your work. I use a site called Fiverr and I found a cover designer and editor for a very good price. Also, please be cautious of companies that say they will publish for you and do all the marketing and you end up spending thousands of dollars before even selling a book. Stay away from these type of deals and companies at all costs!!

In the end there are pros and cons in both avenues, traditional vs self -publish. It is up to you to choose what works better for you and your situation. So please do your research.

I hope all of this was helpful to you. I hope this journey has left you with a big sense of accomplishment and a book in your hands. As I stated earlier, my goal was to take all of the things I learned in my own book writing journey and share it with you, so your process can run nice and smooth. I love you all and I want to wish you the best of luck and say thank you for participating in this course. I can't wait to see your book on the book shelves.

CONGRATULATIONS, YOU ARE NOW OFFICIALLY A WRITER!!!

The Writing Guide Checklist

Please use this portion of the book to help keep track of your progress. This is important in helping you build the momentum to begin and finish your book.

<u>WEEK # 1</u>

Day 1-2: Write your opening paragraph.

Day 3-4: Write your first page.

Day 5-7: Finish your first five pages

<u>WEEK # 2</u>

Day 1-2: Let's write four pages.

Day 3-4: Let's write another four pages

**Day 5-7: Lets ramp up the momentum. Write five pages.
          For a total page count of 18 pages in two weeks.**

<u>WEEK # 3</u>

Day 1-2: Let's write four pages.

Day 3-4: Let's write another five pages

Day 5-7: Lets ramp up the momentum. Write six pages.
For a total page count of 33 pages in three weeks.

WEEK # 4

Day 1-2: Let's write five pages.

Day 3-4: Let's write another six pages

Day 5-7: Lets ramp up the momentum. Write eight pages.
For a total page count of 52 pages in Four weeks.

WEEK # 5

Day 1-2: Let's write five pages.

Day 3-4: Let's write another six pages

Day 5-7: Write eight pages. For a total page count of 71
pages in five weeks.

WEEK # 6

Day 1-2: Let's write five pages.

Day 3-4: Let's write another six pages

Day 5-7: Write eight pages. For a total page count of 90 freaking pages in week six!!

WEEK # 7

Day 1-2: Let's write five pages.

Day 3-4: Let's write another six pages

Day 5-7: Write eight pages. For a total page count of 109 pages in seven weeks.

WEEK # 8

Day 1-2: Let's write six pages.

Day 3-4: Let's write another eight pages

Day 5-7: Write eight pages. For a total page count of 131 pages in eight weeks.

WEEK # 9

Day 1-2: Let's write seven pages.

Day 3-4: Let's write another eight pages

Day 5-7: Write eight pages. For a total page count of 154

pages in nine weeks.

WEEK # 10

Day 1-2: Let's write seven pages.

Day 3-4: Let's write another eight pages

Day 5-7: Write eight pages. For a total page count of 177
pages in ten weeks.

WEEK # 11

Day 1-2: Let's write seven pages.

Day 3-4: Let's write another eight pages

Day 5-7: Finish up eight pages. For a total page count of 200
pages in eleven weeks.

WEEK# 12

Day 1- 2: Put the book down. Take a break and celebrate!

Day 3-7: Reread your book and make any changes in our final
draft.

The Book Outline

Main character (s)

Protagonist (s)

Antagonist (s)

Main Plot of the book

What will the characters go or grow through?

Setting

www.ingramcontent.com/pod-product-compliance
Lightning Source LLC
Chambersburg PA
CBHW021914040426
42447CB00007B/850